T0011276

SHOW AND TELL!

GREAT GRAPHS AND SMART CHARTS

An Introduction to Infographics

TO NANCY, WHO HAS SHOWN ME A LOT AND TOLD
ME MORE AS WE HAVE MADE OUR WAY THROUGH
A WONDERFUL LIFE TOGETHER—**S.J.M.**

TO MY PARENTS—THANK YOU FOR EVERYTHING—**T. B.**

Text copyright © 2022 by Stuart J. Murphy
Illustrations copyright © 2022 by Teresa Bellón

All rights reserved, including the right of reproduction in whole or
in part in any form. Charlesbridge and colophon are registered
trademarks of Charlesbridge Publishing, Inc.

At the time of publication, all URLs printed in this book were
accurate and active. Charlesbridge, the author, and the illustrator
are not responsible for the content or accessibility of any website.

Published by Charlesbridge
9 Galen Street
Watertown, MA 02472
(617) 926-0329
www.charlesbridge.com

Printed in China
(hc) 10 9 8 7 6 5 4 3 2 1
(pb) 10 9 8 7 6 5 4 3 2 1

Illustrations done in digital media
Display type and hand lettering by Teresa Bellón
Text type set in Brandon Grotesque by Hannes von Döhren
Printing by 1010 Printing International Limited in Huizhou,
  Guangdong, China
Production supervision by Jennifer Most Delaney
Designed by Jon Simeon

Library of Congress Cataloging-in-Publication Data

Names: Murphy, Stuart J., 1942– author. | Bellón, Teresa, illustrator.
Title: Show and tell! great graphs and smart charts: an introduction to
  infographics / Stuart J. Murphy; illustrated by Teresa Bellón.
Other titles: Great graphs and smart charts
Description: Watertown, MA: Charlesbridge, [2022] | Summary: "A
  unique introduction to how charts and graphs can present data in
  an easy-to-understand way. Using engaging text and humor, this
  introduction to an otherwise dry mathematics concept explains how
  to show information in chart or graph form in clear terms for young
  readers." —Provided by publisher.
Identifiers: LCCN 2019014211 (print) | LCCN 2019020240 (ebook)
  | ISBN 9781580898232 (reinforced for library use) | ISBN
  9781623541750 (paperback) | ISBN 9781632897114 (ebook)
Subjects: LCSH: Graph theory—Juvenile literature. | Mathematics—
  Juvenile literature.
Classification: LCC QA166 .M87 2022 (print) | LCC QA166 (ebook) |
  DDC 511.5—dc23
LC record available at https://lccn.loc.gov/2019014211
LC ebook record available at https://lccn.loc.gov/2019020240

Graphs and charts show complicated information visually, making it simple and easy to understand. They can help us compare data, follow trends, and make decisions based on facts.

It's often faster and more fun to learn about something from a graph rather than from words or a list of figures.

I LIKE FASTER.

I'M ALL ABOUT FUN!

There are lots of different kinds of charts and graphs.

Here are a few of the most common:

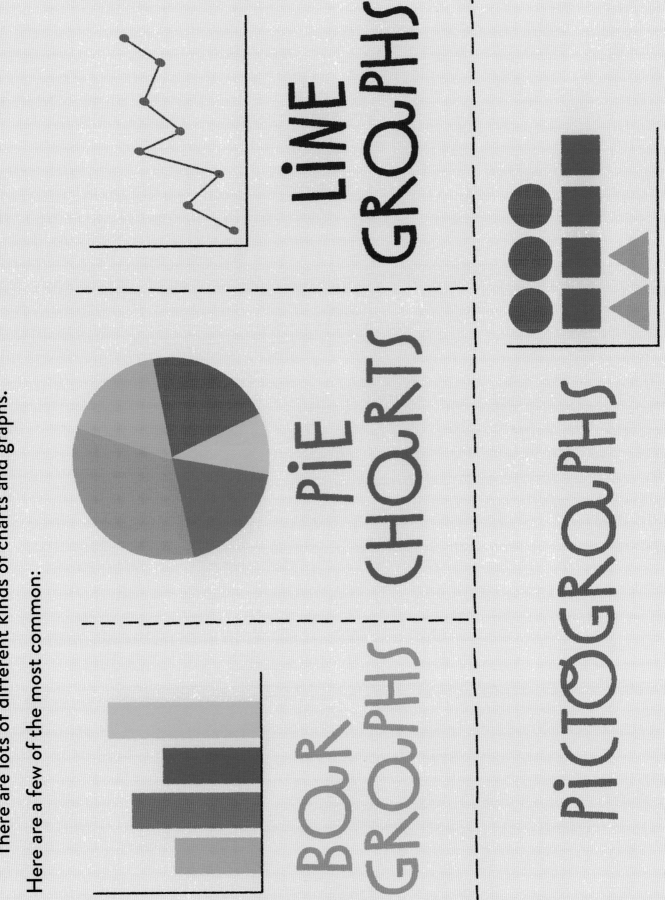

LINE GRAPHS

PIE CHARTS

BAR GRAPHS

PICTOGRAPHS

To make information more exciting and dynamic, graphs and charts are often combined with other visual materials, such as symbols, diagrams, maps, photos, and artwork.

When these are merged with text and other related data, they become what are known as infographics.

THiS WiLL BE GREAT!

In order to create graphs and charts, you need to know how to collect and organize data and then select the kind of graph that will work best for the information.

BAR GRAPHS

Graphs that use parallel bars to show data are called bar graphs.
They are especially good for showing and comparing data that can
easily be separated into items or categories.

It might be fun to know which meal is most popular among
your family and friends. First, make a list of some favorites.

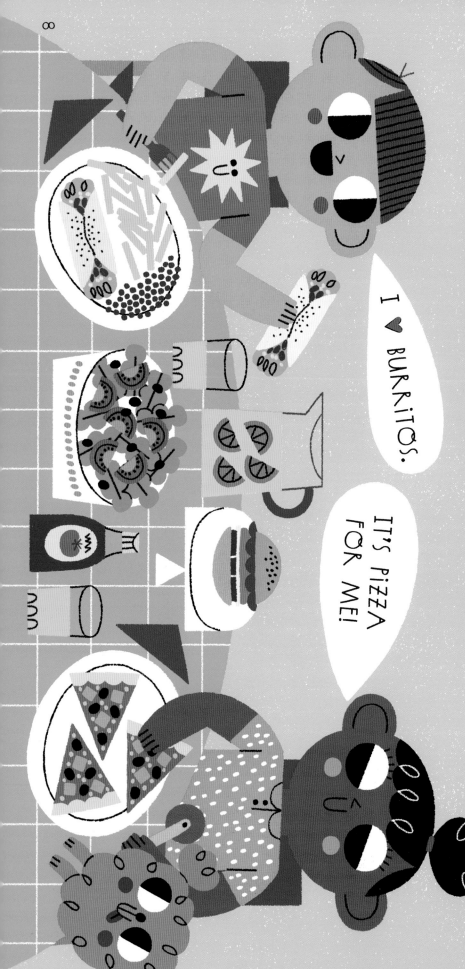

I ♥ BURRITOS.

IT'S PIZZA FOR ME!

Take a poll. Ask everyone you know which of these meals they like best. Keep track with tally marks, and then add them up. You can make a chart, sometimes called a table, to show your data.

ONE VOTE PER PERSON.

DOGS DON'T COUNT!

MEAL	TALLY	TOTAL
MAC 'N' CHEESE	卌 卌	10
PIZZA	卌 卌 卌 卌 I	21
CHICKEN AND RICE	卌 卌 卌	15
SALAD BAR	卌 III	8
BURRITO	卌 卌 卌 III	18
HAMBURGER AND FRIES	卌 卌 III	13

Favorite Meals

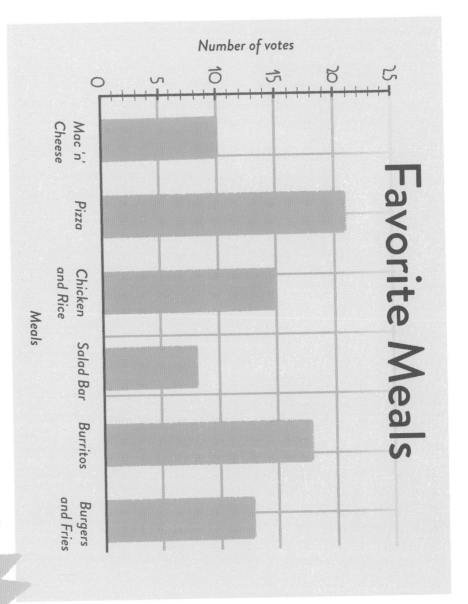

Number of votes

Meals: Mac 'n' Cheese, Pizza, Chicken and Rice, Salad Bar, Burritos, Burgers and Fries

1. Draw a large L on your paper. The vertical line is called the y-axis and the horizontal line is the x-axis.
2. List the meals along the bottom (the x-axis).
3. List the number of votes up the side (the y-axis) by fives (from 0 to 25 with four tick marks in between each number).
4. Use the data you collected and draw bars for each meal.
5. Be sure to add labels and a title.

ADD SOME
SPUNKY TITLE TO
ART AND A
CREATE A TASTY
INFOGRAPHIC.

SALAD BAR IS THE
LEAST FAVORITE MEAL

BURRITOS
CAME IN SECOND.

HOW MANY PEOPLE
PICKED PIZZA
OR BURRITOS?

You can also make horizontal bar graphs. Sometimes that can make it easier to compare the data.

Let's suppose you have a brother and a sister, a mom and dad, and a grandma at home. Each of you has a sheet of paper to keep track of your burps for an entire week. You can use tally marks.

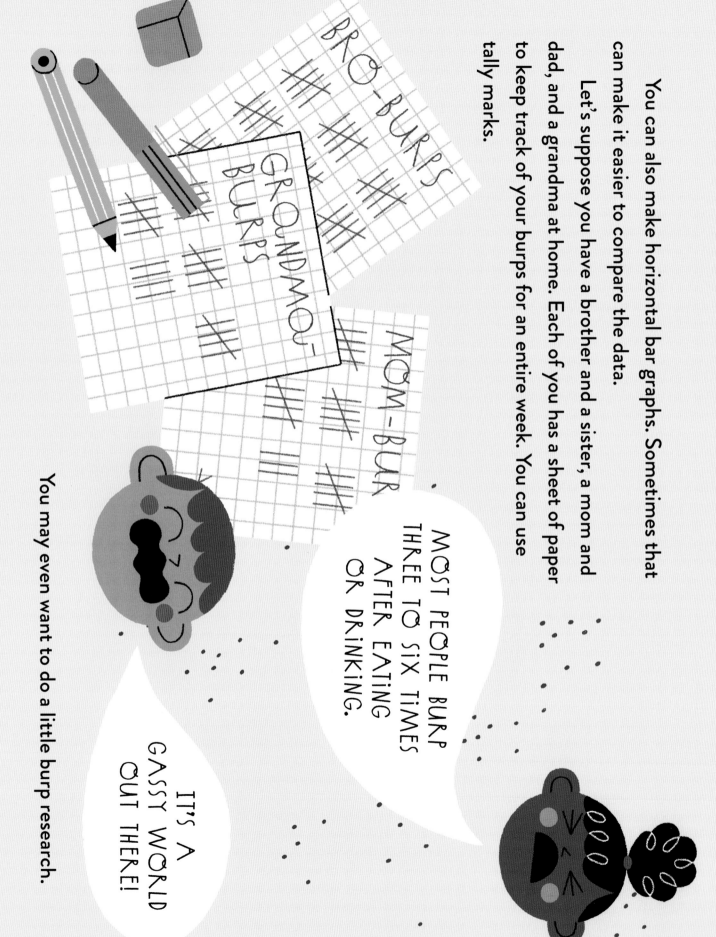

BRO-BURPS

GRANDMOI-BURPS

MOM-BUR...

MOST PEOPLE BURP THREE TO SIX TIMES AFTER EATING OR DRINKING.

IT'S A GASSY WORLD OUT THERE!

You may even want to do a little burp research.

At the end of the week, gather the sheets, total the tally marks, and make a table of your data.

DAD GOT TO 100!

I DON'T THINK GRANDMA COUNTED ALL OF HERS!

PERSON	NUMBER OF BURPS
ME	85
SIS	90
BRO	75
MOM	70
DAD	100
GRANDMA	50

BURRRP!

Now it's time to make your graph.

Number of Burps in a Week

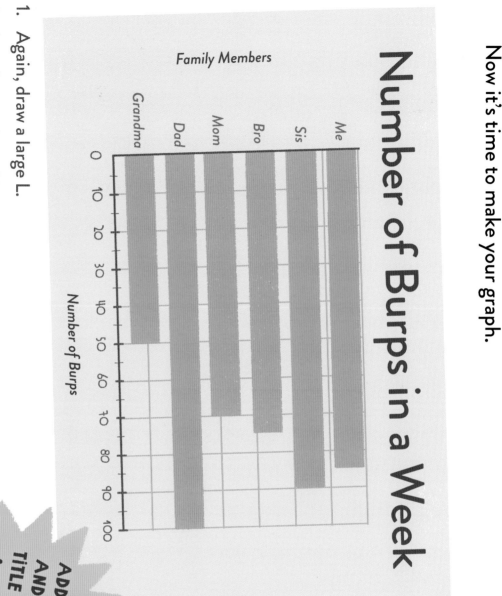

Family Members

Grandma
Dad
Mom
Bro
Sis
Me

0 10 20 30 40 50 60 70 80 90 100

Number of Burps

1. Again, draw a large L.
2. List the number of burps along the bottom at intervals of ten (from 0 to 100 with tick marks halfway in between).
3. List your family members down the side.
4. Be sure to add labels and a title.

ADD SOME ART
AND A SPUNKY
TITLE TO CREATE
A BURP-TASTIC
INFOGRAPHIC.

IT LOOKS LIKE DAD
IS THE BURP KING
OF THE FAMILY.

HOW MANY MORE
BURPS DID DAD HAVE
THAN MOM?

HOW MANY BURPS
WERE THERE IN ALL?
THERE SURE WERE
A LOT!

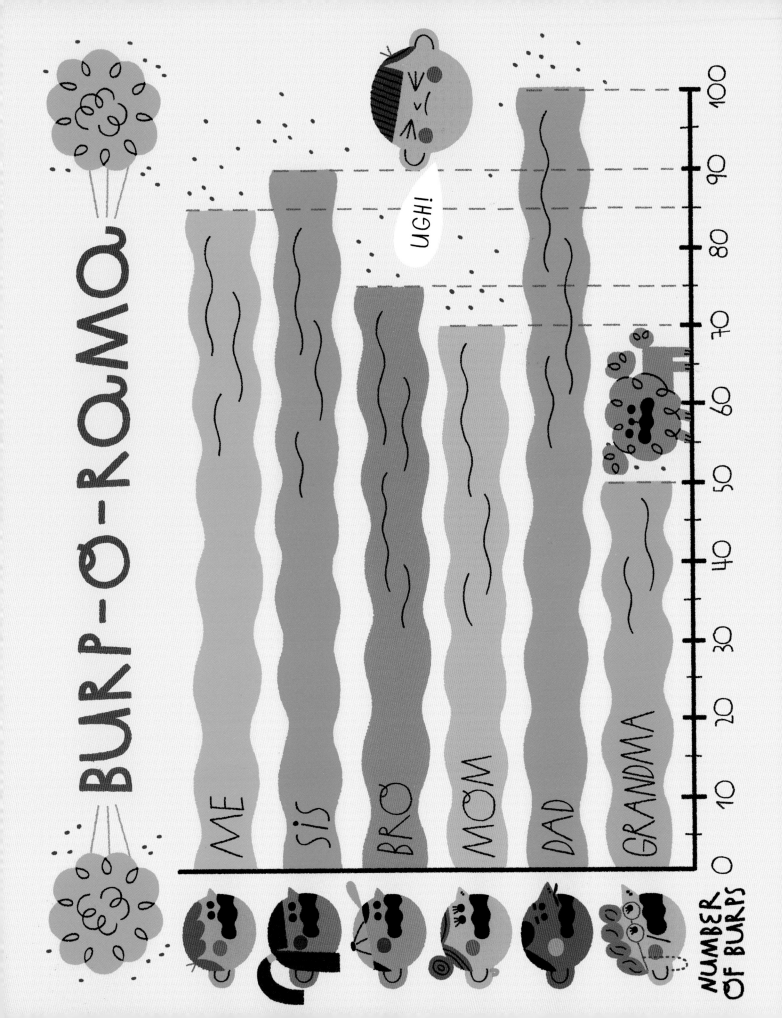

PICTOGRAPHS

Pictographs use pictures to represent the data shown on a graph.

Let's say the members of your science club want to know which are the most common household pets in your school. Recent statistics show that in the United States fish are at the top of the list. That's because people usually own more than one fish at a time! After fish, the four most common pets are cats, dogs, birds, and hamsters or other small mammals.

I WONDER WHICH OF THESE FIVE ARE THE MOST COMMON HERE?

THERE MAY BE SOMETHING FISHY GOING ON!

The students made a chart. In the first column, they listed the five most popular pets in alphabetical order. They created pictures of each pet. After visiting every classroom, they found that the pet populations of these five pets in their schools' families came out like this:

I FOUND A FAMILY WITH ALL FIVE PETS.

THAT SOUNDS LIKE A ZOO!

PETS	PICTURES	APPROXIMATE QUANTITIES
BIRDS	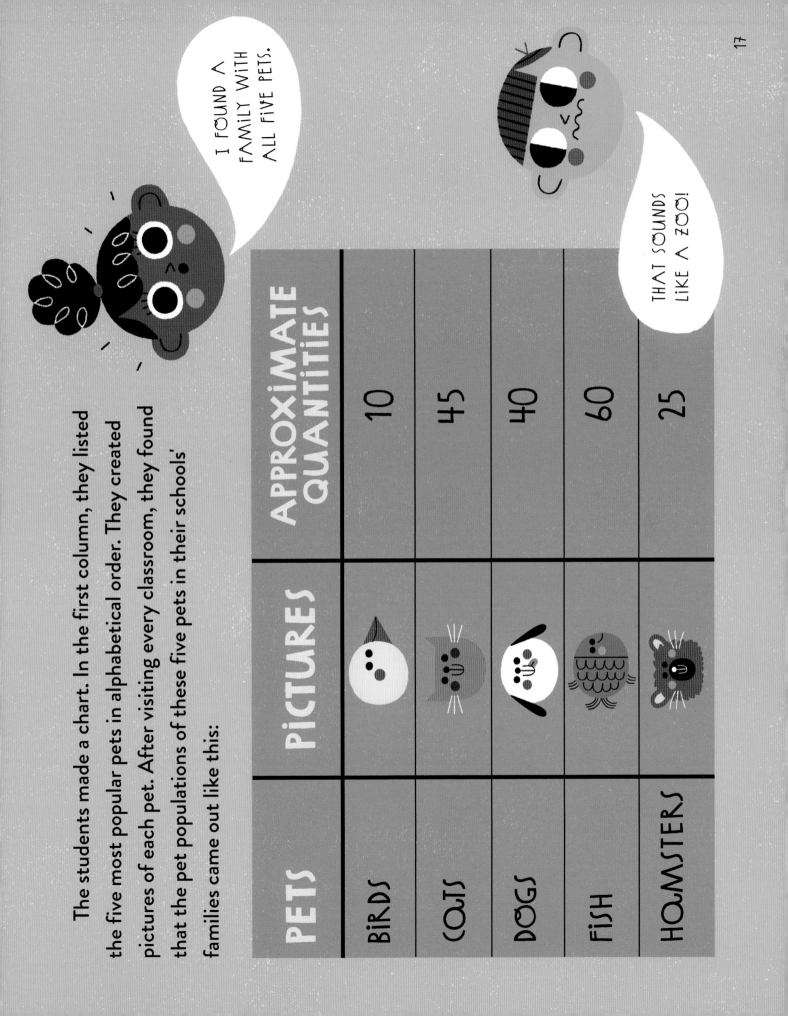	10
CATS		45
DOGS		40
FISH		60
HAMSTERS		25

Most Common Pets in Our School

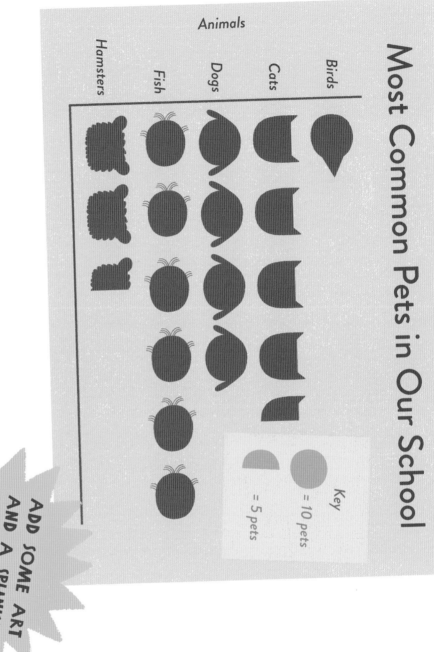

Animals

- Birds
- Cats
- Dogs
- Fish
- Hamsters

Key

= 10 pets

= 5 pets

ADD SOME ART
AND A SPUNKY
TITLE TO CREATE
A PET-FRIENDLY
INFOGRAPHIC.

1. Draw a large L on a blank piece of paper.
2. List the pets down the side and draw pictures of the animals in a row.
3. Include a key showing that each full picture represents ten pets and each half picture represents five.
4. Be sure to add labels and a title.

HOW MANY FEWER DOGS THAN CATS DID THE FAMILIES HAVE?

HOW MUCH OF A DIFFERENCE IS THERE BETWEEN THE LEAST AND MOST COMMON PET?

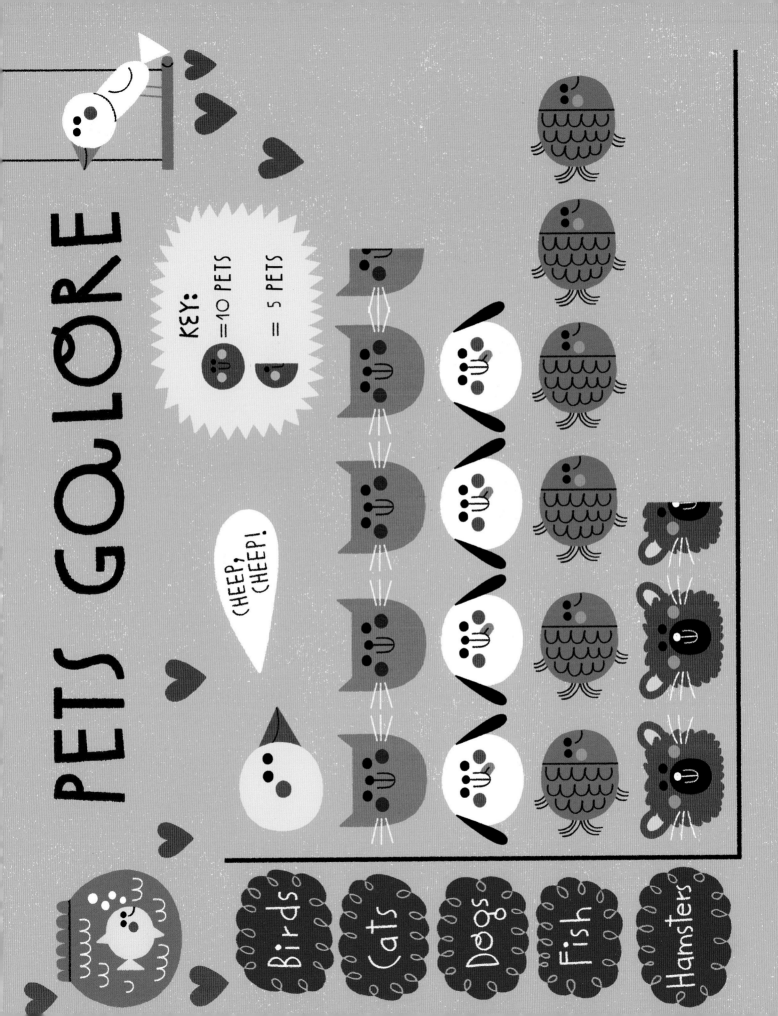

PiE CHARTS

Pie charts, also called circle graphs, are graphs in the shape of a circle that show how a whole is broken into parts. They can be used to compare categories that make up a whole. Each segment of the pie chart represents a fraction of the whole.

Suppose you and your friends have decided to spend the day at an amusement park. The sign above the entrance shows three types of rides.

OUTER SPACE PARK
DATA COLLECTION

IT'S GOING TO BE HARD TO PICK.

OUTER SPACE PARK	40 RIDES
GALAXY RIDES — WILD AND SCARY	10
COSMIC RIDES — FAST AND FUN	10
ASTRO RIDES — NICE AND EASY	20

GALAXY RIDES
COSMIC RIDES
ASTRO RIDES

Of the forty rides, 10 of 40, or $\frac{1}{4}$, are Wild and Scary. Another 10 of 40, also $\frac{1}{4}$, are Fast and Fun. And 20 of 40, or $\frac{1}{2}$, are Nice and Easy.

NOT FOR ME. THE SCARIER, THE BETTER!

Outer Space Park Rides

You can show the different categories by creating a pie chart.

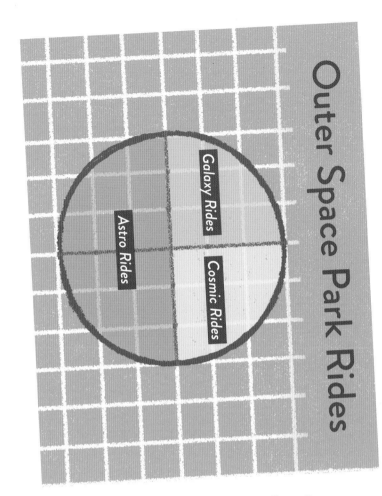

Galaxy Rides

Astro Rides

Cosmic Rides

1. Draw a big circle. You may want to trace a small plate or glass or something else that's round.

2. Make a straight line down the middle to create two half segments. Make a straight line across the middle to create four quarter segments.

3. Make two segments one color to show the Astro Rides and the other two segments two different colors to show the Galaxy and the Cosmic Rides.

4. Be sure to add labels and a title.

ADD SOME ART AND A SPUNKY TITLE TO CREATE A STELLAR INFOGRAPHIC.

MAYBE I CAN TRY RIDES IN ALL THREE GROUPS.

WHAT IF FIVE OF THE GALAXY RIDES WERE IN ANOTHER CATEGORY: SCARIEST OF THEM ALL?

THAT WOULD BE 5 OF 40 RIDES, OR $\frac{1}{8}$. AND I'D BE FIRST IN LINE!

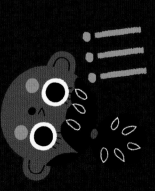

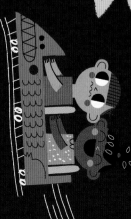

Now let's try a pie chart using percentages. A percentage is a way of expressing a fraction when the whole is 100 equal parts. Each segment of the pie chart represents a percent of the whole, or a number out of 100. The total segments must add up to 100. A percentage is followed by the percent sign: %.

Assume there are 100 kids signed up for a town athletic program. The program director has asked everyone to select one of four sports. The choices are basketball, swimming, soccer, and track.

The number of kids who signed up for each of the choices is posted. The number is also shown as a percent. For example, 40 out of 100 is the same as the fraction $\frac{40}{100}$, which is 40%.

SOCCER ALL THE WAY!

THAT'S A LOT OF KIDS. AND A LOT OF FUN!

SPORT	NUMBER OF KIDS	FRACTION	PERCENT
SOCCER	40	$\frac{40}{100}$	40%
TRACK	30	$\frac{30}{100}$	30%
BASKETBALL	20	$\frac{20}{100}$	20%
SWIMMING	10	$\frac{10}{100}$	10%
TOTALS	100	$\frac{100}{100}$	100%

Show the results by creating a pie chart.

Athletic Program Selections

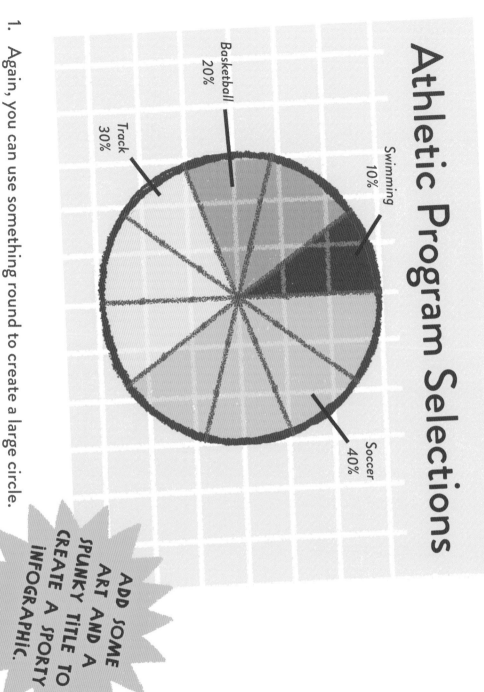

Swimming
10%

Basketball
20%

Track
30%

Soccer
40%

1. Again, you can use something round to create a large circle.
2. Divide the circle into ten equal parts. Each part represents 10%.
3. Use four different colors to show the percentages for each sport.
4. Be sure to add labels and a title.

ADD SOME
ART AND A
SPUNKY TITLE TO
CREATE A SPORTY
INFOGRAPHIC.

WHICH SPORT HAS
THE MOST PARTICIPATION

WHICH SPORT
IS HALF OF
BASKETBALL'S PERCENT?

YOU CAN TELL HOW
THE SPORTS COMPARE
JUST BY LOOKING
AT THE CHART.

ALL ABOUT SPORTS

SOCCER 40%

TRACK 30%

SWIMMING 10%

BASKETBALL 20%

LINE GRAPHS

Line graphs can show things that change over time, like the number of miles traveled during a trip, temperature changes throughout the seasons, or the population of a town or city over a number of years. They can be helpful in showing patterns and predicting trends.

Suppose your family is going to visit your cousins. You really want to see them, but it takes the better part of the day to get there.

LET'S HIT THE ROAD!

A great way to pass some time would be to create a line graph of the trip.

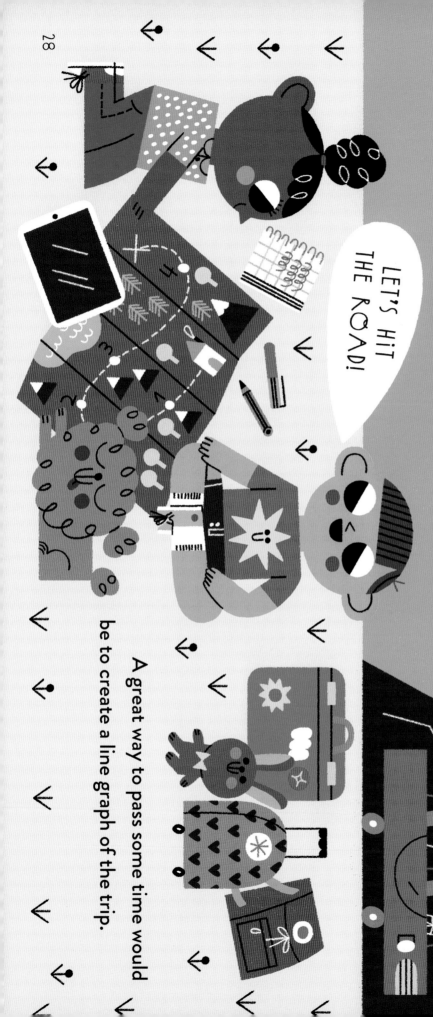

THE TOTAL DISTANCE IS CALCULATED BY ADDING EACH NEW HOUR'S MILES TO THE PREVIOUS HOUR'S TOTAL TRIP DISTANCE.

First you'll have to collect data. You can check the distance traveled for each one-hour leg of the trip on the car's odometer. Then make a table or chart with three columns, one for time period, one for the approximate distance traveled each hour, and one for the total distance traveled.

Your chart might look something like this:

TIME PERIOD	HOURLY DISTANCE IN MILES	TOTAL MILES TRAVELED
8:00 – 9:00	40	40
9:00 – 10:00	60	100
10:00 – 11:00	40	140
11:00 – 12:00	60	200
12:00 – 1:00	0	200
1:00 – 2:00	50	250
2:00 – 3:00	70	320
3:00 – 4:00	30	350

Our Trip Time and Distance

Let's use a piece of graph paper for this one.

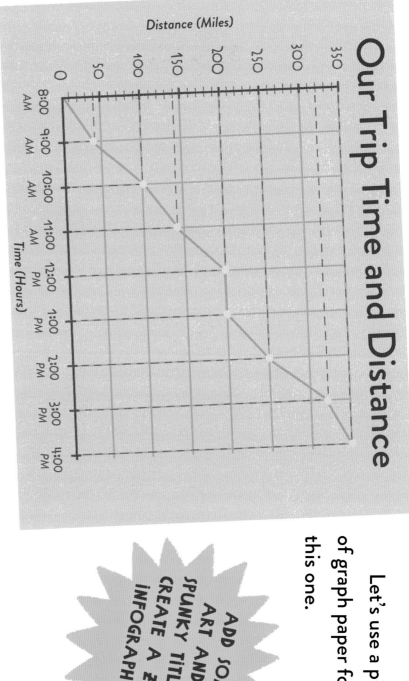

Distance (Miles)

Time (Hours)

1. Make a big L shape.

2. List the hours from 8:00 a.m. to 4:00 p.m. along the x-axis and the miles from 0 to 350 at fifty-mile intervals with tick marks for every ten miles on the y-axis.

3. Use the data you collected to make a graph. Mark the points on the graph and then connect them with lines. You may want to use a ruler.

4. Be sure to add labels and a title.

ADD SOME SPUNKY ART AND A CREATE A ZIPPY TITLE TO INFOGRAPHIC.

WHY IS THE LINE BETWEEN 2:00 AND 3:00 STEEPER THAN THE LINE BETWEEN 3:00 AND 4:00?

WHERE IS THE LINE FLAT? WHY?

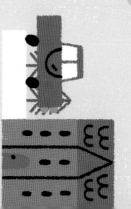

THE STEEPER OUR LINE, THE FASTER WE'RE GOING

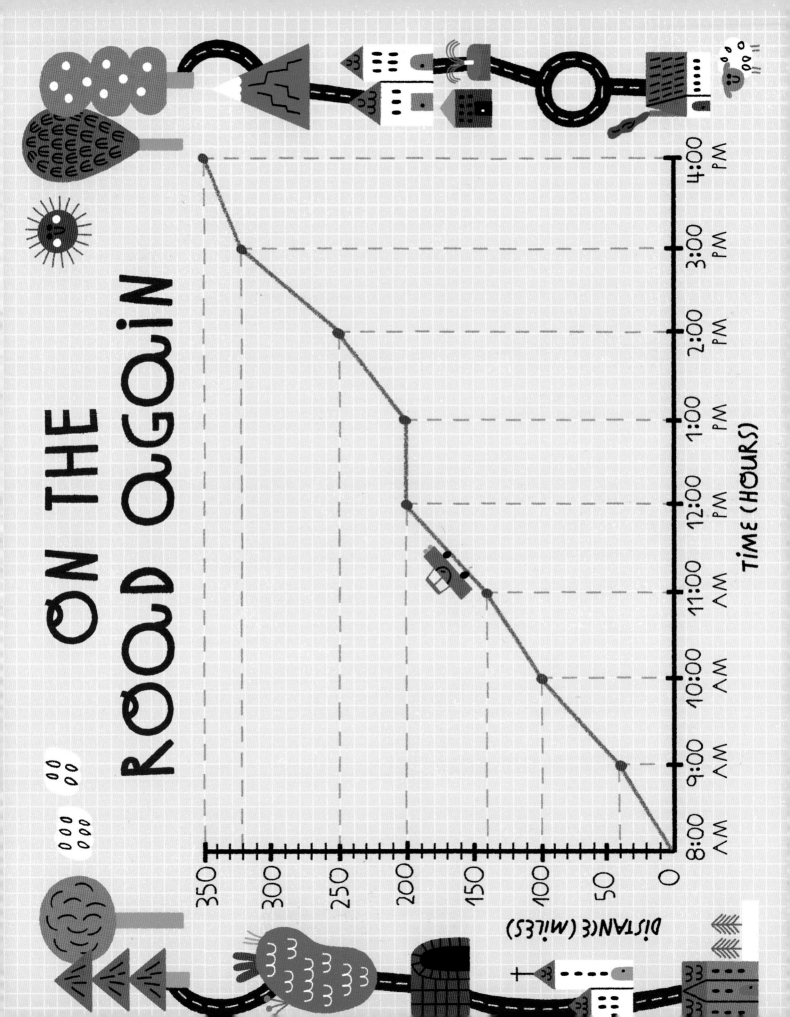

ON THE
ROAD AGAIN

TIME (HOURS)

8:00 AM 9:00 AM 10:00 AM 11:00 AM 12:00 PM 1:00 PM 2:00 PM 3:00 PM 4:00 PM

DISTANCE (MILES)

0 50 100 150 200 250 300 350

Line graphs can go up and down depending on the increases and decreases in the data that has been collected. They could show the number of people at an event at different times or compare the sales of products over a period of time.

Let's say your school is having an all-morning field day. It starts at 9:00 a.m., and people will come and go until 12:00 p.m., when a big picnic lunch is served.

PICNICS ARE GREAT!

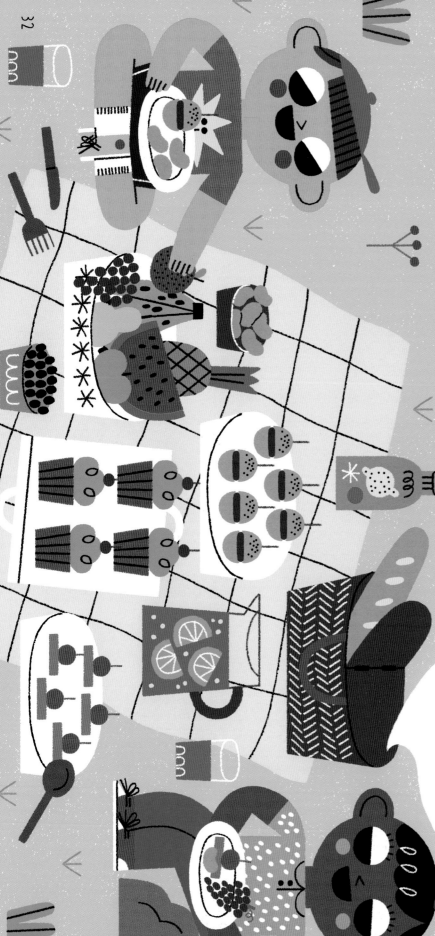

A maximum of 600 people are allowed on the field at any one time. In order to keep track, you and a buddy could stand near the entrance. One of you could count the people coming in, and the other could count the people going out.

WOW! THAT'S A LOT OF PEOPLE!

ARE WE GETTING CLOSE TO MAXIMUM CAPACITY?

TIME	IN	OUT
9:00 – 9:30	150	0
9:30 – 10:00	275	75
10:00 – 10:30	100	250
10:30 – 11:00	225	75
11:00 – 11:30	250	50
11:30 – 12:00	50	100

Now find the difference for each half hour and add that
to the total attendance.

TIME INTERVAL	IN	OUT	DIFFERENCE	TOTAL
9:00 – 9:30	150	0	+150	150
9:30 – 10:00	275	75	+200	350
10:00 – 10:30	100	250	-150	200
10:30 – 11:00	225	75	+150	350
11:00 – 11:30	250	50	+200	550
11:30 – 12:00	50	100	-50	500

Field Day Attendance

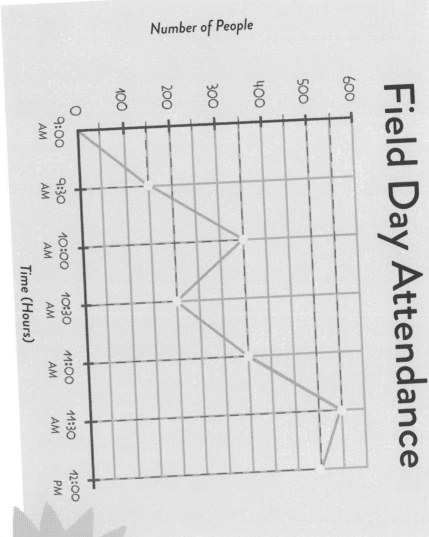

Number of People

600
500
400
300
200
100
0

9:00 AM · 9:30 AM · 10:00 AM · 10:30 AM · 11:00 AM · 11:30 AM · 12:00 PM

Time (Hours)

1. Again, draw a big L shape.
2. List the time intervals along the x-axis and the number of people on the y-axis from 0 to 600 at intervals of 100 with a tick mark at each 50.
3. Use the information in the chart to create your graph. Mark the points. Then connect the points with lines.
4. Be sure to add labels and a title.

ADD SOME ART AND A SPUNKY TITLE TO CREATE A FRESH INFOGRAPHIC.

WHAT TWO TIME INTERVALS HAD THE SAME ATTENDANCE?

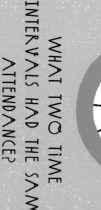

WHEN WERE THERE THE MOST PEOPLE ON THE FIELD?

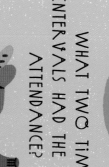

WHAT WOULD HAPPEN IF WE HAD ANOTHER HOUR? WE'D BE TURNING FOLKS AWAY.

You may want to try more graphs on your own about topics that interest you. The possibilities are endless. Do your research, note your sources, organize your information, plan your visuals, and create! There are programs online for drawing graphs and charts, or you can make them by hand.

Remember: In addition to graphs and charts, an infographic can include pictures, maps, lists—anything that helps to explain or enhance the information that you want to show and tell the world. You could even build an infographic about you—a self-portrait or visual biography that tells everyone all about who you are. Include your name and lots of visual information.

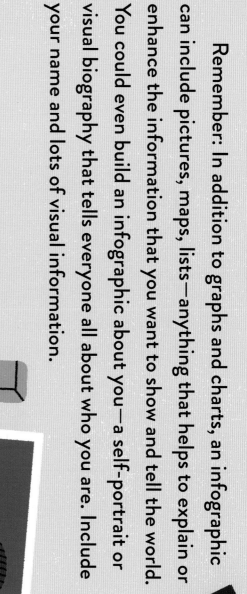
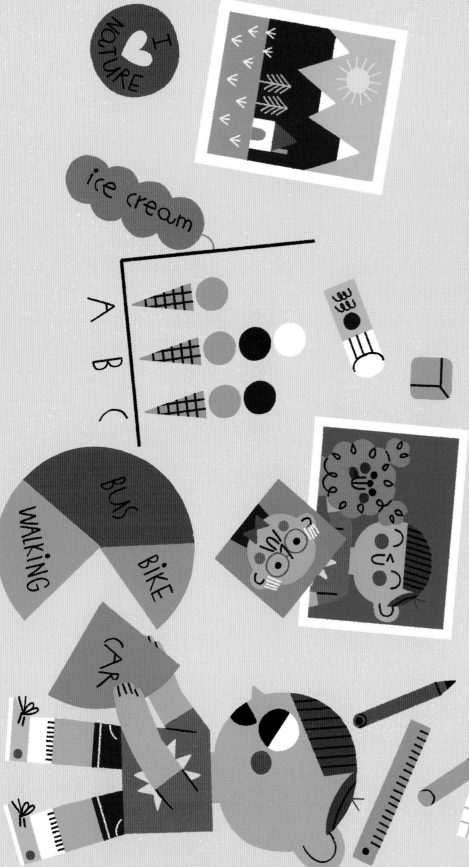

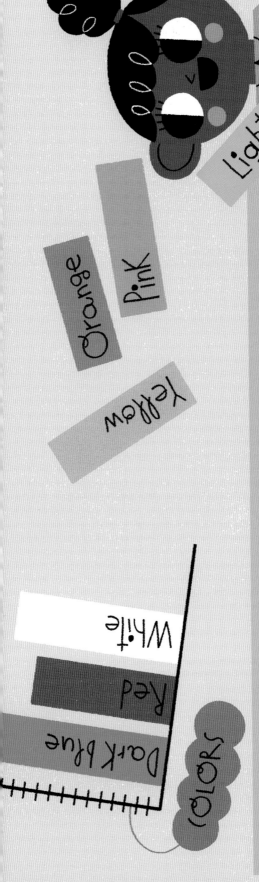

INFOGRAPHIC IDEAS

- A pie chart showing the percent of kids that come to school by car, bus, bike, or walking. Make sure they add up to 100%.

- A photo of a special place.

- A line graph of your longest trip, bike ride, or run.

- A picture of your family. Don't forget your pets!

- A map from your house to a friend's house.

- Photos of your best friends.

- A pictograph of favorite ice cream flavors among a group of your friends.

- A line graph showing your change in height over time.

- A drawing of what you want to be when you grow up.

- A bar graph that shows the top five favorite colors in your classroom.

- Whatever pops into your head!